SUMMER SUNDAY

A comical-tragical-ecological Pastoral
for SATB, piano and double bass

words by
GORDON SNELL

music by
JOSEPH HOROVITZ

NOVELLO PUBLISHING LIMITED

Order No: NOV 200174

Commissioned by the Cookham Festival Society with funds made available by the Arts Council of Great Britain, and first performed at Holy Trinity Church on 28 May 1975 conducted by Sara Wood.

NOTES ON PERFORMANCE

Indications like 'solo', 'small group' or 'all' etc are to be regarded only as suggestions, and conductors will no doubt vary the distribution of parts among the singers according to the talents available. Any solo which bears a 'character-name' like 'cow' or 'crow' etc. may be sung by any type of voice regardless of pitch (clef), but it is advisable to plan the performance so that certain singers retain a 'role' throughout the piece, rather as in an opera.

The work seems to cry out for some sort of staging, or semi-staging, but I should like to remind producers that movement on a stage often tends to interfere with tempo markings; this should be avoided at all cost.

Although *Summer Sunday* has a serious message about the preservation of our countryside, this will come across to the audience all the more if a sense of fun is always retained by all participants.

Double bass

This part is available from the publisher. It is optional, but I regard it as essential for a really successful performance.

JOSEPH HOROVITZ

DURATION 37 MINUTES

SUMMER SUNDAY

ORDON SNELL

JOSEPH HOROVITZ

20171

1
Sun - day, one day luz - ing,
Sun - day, one day luz - ing,
Sun - day, one day luz - ing,
Sun - day, one day luz - ing,
1
cresc.
sun - light blaz - ing, sun-ny sum-mer Sun - day,
sun - light blaz - ing, sun-ny sum-mer Sun - day,
sun - light blaz - ing, sun-ny sum-mer Sun - day,
sun - light blaz - ing, sun-ny sum-mer Sun - day,
cresc.
mf
p
Sun - day. Sun - day,
pp
Sun - day.
ah
Sun - day.
ah
Sun - day. ah

2
Sun - day,
sun-ny sum-mer
ah
ah
ah
ah
ah
ah
2
Sun - day,
one day
luz - ing,
one day
luz - ing,
ah
one day
luz - ing,
ah
ah
3
cresc.
sun - light
blaz - ing,
sun-ny
sum-mer
Sun - day,
cresc.
sun - light
blaz - ing,
sun - ny
sum-mer
Sun - day,
cresc.
sun - light
blaz - ing,
sun - ny
sum-mer
Sun - day,
cresc.
ah
ah
3
cresc.

mf
p
Sun - day.
Sun - day.
Sun - day,
Sun - day.
ah
Sun - day.
mf
p
move a little
SOLO I
♩=100
mf
Out there in the
poco cresc.
mf
4
coun - try - side the trees grow just where they de - cide,
p smooth
no sound but the wind, and the gur - gle of the stream,
p
pp
Ped.
✱ (soft Ped. only)
L.H. poco marcato

(SOLO I)
FULL
S mf
no high wall and no hard street, on-ly grass, green
A mf
on-ly grass, green
T
B
mf
5
grass, on-ly green, green grass, on-ly green grass.
mf
p
And the on-ly light is the light of the sun, the on-ly light is the
the on-ly light is the

light of the sun in the free, wide, la - zy air of the coun - try - side,
light of the sun in the free, wide, la - zy air of the coun - try - side,
in the free, wide, la - zy air of the coun - try - side,
6
the free, wide, lu - zy air of the coun - try - side,
the free, wide, lu - zy air of the coun - try - side,
the free, wide, lu - zy air of the coun - try - side,
6
the coun - try - side.
the coun - try - side.
the coun - try - side.

7
p
Sun - day,
p
Sun - day,
p
Sun - day,
7
sun-ny sum-mer Sun - day,
sun-ny sum-mer Sun - day,
p
Sun - day, Sun - - - day,
p
sun-ny sum-mer,
one day laz - ing, sun - light blaz - ing,
one day laz - ing, sun - light blaz - ing,
one day laz - ing, sun - light blaz - ing,
one day laz - ing, sun - light blaz - ing,

8
poco ritard.
sun-ny sum-mer Sun - day,
pp
sun-ny sum-mer Sun - day, Sun - day,
pp
sun-ny sum-mer Sun - day, Sun - day,
pp
sun-ny sum-mer Sun - day, Sun - day,
8
poco ritard.
molto ritard.
Sun - day,
p
Sun - day,
p
Sun - day, Sun - day,
p
Sun - day, Sun - day,
molto ritard.
p
pp strict tempo ♩=80
sun-ny sum-mer Sun-day.
pp
sun-ny sum-mer Sun-day.
ppp
Sun - day.
ppp
Sun - day.
strict tempo ♩=80
pp

9 Fast ♩= 132
f
L.H.
SOLO I
f
Where's the pic-nic bas - ket?
SOLO II
Where's my sum-mer
mf
simile
hat?
SOLO III
Where's the fold-ing tab - le?
SOLO IV
Don't for-
get to feed the cat!
SOLO V
10
Where's the Sun-day pa - per?
SOLO VI
Where's my ra-di-
o?
SOLO VII
Where's the co-ca - co - la? And the brand-y for Aunt Flo!
cresc.

SOLO I
f
Where's the sun - tan
f
mf
SOLO II
mf
SOLO III
f
11
SOLO IV
mf
SOLO V
f
lo - tion? Fly - spray! Where's my plas - tic mac? Got the tea-bugs? Don't for-
SOLO VI
mf
f
SOLO VII
get the pot of jel - ly! Lock the door! Turn off the tel - ly! Where's
L.H.
SOLO VI
SOLO I
the bot - tle op'-ner? Did you find the ra - di - o? Where's the black um-

FULL
S
brel-lu? And the brand-y for Aunt Flo! Oh no! Don't for-get the brand-y -
A
And the brand-y for Aunt Flo! Oh no! Don't for-get the brand-y -
T
And the brand-y for Aunt Flo! Oh no! Don't for-get the brand-y -
B
And the brand-y for Aunt Flo! Oh no! Don't for-get the brand-y -
12
flask for Aunt-ie Flo!
flask for Aunt-ie Flo!
flask for Aunt-ie Flo!
flask for Aunt-ie Flo!
12
brillante
steadier ♩=120
Start the car!
Start the car!
Start the car!
Start the car!
Start the car!
Start the car!
steadier ♩=120

And off we go in - to the coun-try, off we go
And off we go in - to the coun-try, off we go
And off we go in - to the coun-try, off we go
And off we go in - to the coun-try, off we go
ff
mf
simile
13
mf
in the car, on our way in - to the coun-try, on our way
in the car, on our way in - to the coun-try, on our way
in the car, on our way in - to the coun-try, on our way
in the car, on our way in - to the coun-try, on our way,
13
p
in the car; now
in the car; now
in the car; now
on our way in the car; now

14

p

off we go into the country, off we go in the car,

off we go into the country, off we go in the car,

off we go into the country, off we go in the car,

off we go into the country, off we go in the car,

14

p

out of town, into the country, in the car.

out of town, into the country, in the car.

out of town, into the country, in the car.

out of town, into the country, in the car.

15
15
soft Ped. only
SOLO I
mf
Got the deck-chairs?
SOLO II
mf
Left my
knit-ting!
16
SOLO III
mf
Got the blank-et?
SOLO IV
(a beery voice) mf
The
beer
cans!

SOLO V (child)
p
pp
Sponge - cake!
17
pp
p cresc.
f
f
senza Ped.
SMALL GROUP I mf
One mile,
SMALL GROUP II pp
Sun-ny sum-mer Sun-day,
p
SMALL GROUP III mf
two miles,
SMALL GROUP IV pp
Sun-ny sum-mer Sun-day,
SMALL GROUP I mf
three miles,
SMALL GROUP II pp
Sun-ny sum-mer Sun-day,

18
FULL
S A T B
mf
ritard.
cresc.
four miles!
f
slow march ♩ = 80
We're stuck! We're stuck like a clam! In a
traf-fic jam! Oh damn! This traf-fic jam! And
20171

19
move a bit ♩=96
all the Sun - day driv - ers! Damn!
all the Sun - day driv - ers! Damn!
all the Sun - day driv - ers! Damn!
all the Sun - day driv - ers! Damn
19
move a bit ♩=96
f
mf fed up
The sun comes out and they all come out like
mf fed up
The sun comes out and they all come out like
mf
kazoos ad lib.
f
Beep, barp, beep, barp!
f
Beep, barp, beep, barp!
sheep!
mf
Nose to tail on the
sheep!
mf
Nose to tail on the
f
p

20
Beep, burp, beep, burp!
Beep, burp, beep, burp!
Sun-day trail we creep! They
Sun-day trail we creep! They
20
all come out on the Sun-day trail, bum-per to bum-per, They
all come out on the Sun-day trail, bum-per to bum-per,
SOLO
poco ten.
We creep like sheep, and
We creep like sheep, and
ought to go by rail! FULL We creep like sheep, and
like sheep, and
poco ten.

fast ♩=160
21
beep, beep, brrr, beep, beep, brrr!
Beep!
beep, beep, brrr, beep, beep, brrr!
Beep!
beep, brrr, beep, beep, brrr!
Beep!
SOLO
(deep male voice)
beep,
Look at the fool in front! He's gone to sleep!
fast ♩=160
21
Beep!
Beep!
Beep!
Is that a car he's got? An old junk-heap! I'd like to clear this lot
Wham!
Damn!
Wham!
Wham!
Damn!
with a but-ter-ing-ram! They're not fit to be in charge of a ba-by's pram!

mf
You! Move!
mf
Fool! Fool! You!
mf
FULL
You! Move!
mf
Fool! Fool! You!
mf
22
f
Fool! Move!
f
Move!
f
Fool! Move!
f
Move! Beep!.
22
cresc.
ff
f ff
Burp! Barp! Ba-barp!
f ff
Barp! Burp! Ba-burp!
f ff
Beep! Burp! Barp!
ff
Burp! Burp!
p
ff
mf

23
long
long
p resigned
When
long
long
p resigned
When
23
long
p
mf
with trad. lilt ♩=60
mf
and
mf
I take the high road, and you take the high road, and he takes the high road, and
mf
and he takes the high road, and
mf
I take the high road, and you take the high road, and he takes the high road, and
with trad. lilt ♩=60
p
24
she takes the high road, they all take the high road, the whole lot's driv-ing on
she takes the high road, they all take the high road, the whole lot's driv-ing on
she takes the high road, they all take the high road, the whole lot's driv-ing on
she takes the high road, they all take the high road, the whole lot's driv-ing on
24
mf

my road! There's room on the by-road, so why_ drive on my road, when
my_ road! There's room on the by-road, so why drive on my road, when
my_ road! There's room on the by-road, so why drive on my road, when
my road! There's room on the by-road, so why_ drive on my road, when
move on ♩=120
I took the high road be-fore ye? Beep! Beep! Let's go!
I took the high road be-fore_ ye? Beep! Beep! Let's go!
I took the high road be-fore_ ye? Beep! Beep!
I took the high road be-fore ye?_ Beep! Beep!
move on ♩=120
25
we move,
we move,
At last,
At last,_ at last!_
25

p dreamy
Sun - day,
Sun - day,
p dreamy
Sun - day,
Sun - day,
pp
simile
p
Sun - ny,
sum - mer
p
Sun - ny,
sum - mer

26
Sun - day.
Sun - duy.
26
ppp
molto ritard.
free time
pp SOLO
Sponge - cake...
p SOLO
Left my knit-ting...
molto ritard.
free time
p
no Ped.
moderate ♩=120
ALL f
SOLO I
27
ALL
Here we are! Park the car! Here we are in the
mf

steady ♩= 90
SOLO III
mf
coun-try-side.
Look! There's a tree!
mf SOLO II
SOLO I
Look! There's a farm!
Look! There's a
steady ♩= 90
p
pp
p SOLO II
bird coo-ing, coo-ing, do-ing just what a bird should be
pp
28
SOLO III
mf
SOLO I
mf
do-ing!
Look! There's a stream! Look! There's a
6
p
6
mp
p
Ped.
*
SOLO II
mf
SOLO III
pp
SOLO IV (low voice)
mf
field! Look! There's a cow! Moo-ing, moo-ing – do-ing just what a cow should be
pp

SMALL GROUP I
f
do - ing! How now, brown cow!
mf
sonoro
mf
29
How do you make your milk? Brown cow!
mf
COW SOLO intellectually
f
3
I make it out of a cloud, that's how!
SMALL GROUP I
mf
But how can a cloud make
f
mf
ALL
ff
COW
mf
mf
milk? Brown cow! I'm going to tell you how, right now!
f
p
mf
f

30
♩= 96
mf
There's a cloud in the sky, please con-firm my ob-ser-va-tion;
mf
FULL
f
COW
FULL
There's a cloud in the sky! 'H-2-O' we spe-ci-fy! From the cloud
There's a cloud in the sky! From the cloud
There's a cloud in the sky! From the cloud
There's a cloud in the sky! From the cloud
31
COW
comes the rain! You re-fer to con-den-sa-tion, which de-pends, as we know,
comes the rain!
comes the rain!
comes the rain!
31

FULL
COW
on the temp-'ra - ture be-low. From the earth grows the grass! Fer - ti - lised by
From the earth grows the grass!
From the earth grows the grass!
From the earth grows the grass!
32
più f
pol - lin - a - tion, and the sun, we sur - mise, makes it pho - to - syn - the - size.
FULL
p
mf COW
Then the cow eats the grass! That we call re - gur - gi - ta - tion; for the cud,
Then the cow eats the grass!
Then the cow eats the grass!
Then the cow eats the grass!

f 33 FULL f

ful-ly chewed, makes the best di - ges-ted food! Then the cow starts to moo!

f

Then the cow starts to moo!

f

Then the cow starts to moo!

f

Then the cow starts to moo!

33

f

mf COW

That is bo - vine con - ver - sa - tion! Ve - ry com - fort - ing as well,

p

34 f FULL *impatient*

when the glands be - gin to swell! Have we come to the milk?

f *impatient*

Have we come to the milk?

f *impatient*

Have we come to the milk?

f *impatient*

Have we come to the milk?

34

mf

30
COW
FULL
Yes, by pro-cess of lac-ta-tion! With a squeeze, and a pull,
With a squeeze, and a pull,
With a squeeze, and a pull,
With a squeeze, and a pull,
ff COW
now we've got a buck-et full! And that is how the clouds make your milk!
now we've got a buck-et full!
now we've got a buck-et full!
now we've got a buck-et full!
35 FULL
+ COW
cresc.
Thank you for your ex-pla-na-tion! That's how clouds make your milk!
Thank you for your ex-pla-na-tion! That's how clouds make your milk!
Thank you for your ex-pla-na-tion! That's how clouds make your milk!
Thank you for your ex-pla-na-tion! That's how clouds make your milk!
35
Ped.

speed up
36
ff
Drink a pint-a, drink a pint-a, drink a lit-re ev - 'ry day!
Drink a pint-a, drink a pint-a, drink a lit-re ev - 'ry day!
Drink a pint-a, drink a pint-a, drink a lit-re ev - 'ry day!
Drink a pint-a, drink a pint-a, drink a lit-re ev - 'ry day!
speed up
fff
Moderato ♩ = 60
mp SOLO IV (low voice)
So the brown cow on the green grass stands and
mp
p
mun-ches, as she gaz - es at the peo-ple eat-ing pic-nic
slightly quicker ♩ = 72
lunch-es, and Mum picks up crumbs when the pic-nic's done. and
mf > p
pp

37
p (aside, to audience)
Gran-ny goes to sleep in the hot sun, They're all fit to burst, and Dad's got a thirst, and
sonoro
lilting ♩=90
goes to find a Pub, for a quick one!
p
mp
poco rubato
FULL
a tempo
S
mf
And the child - ren go ex -
A
T
B
poco rubato
a tempo
Ped.

38
plo - ring, in the sum-mer coun - try - side, they're walk - ing in the
plo - ring, in the sum-mer coun - try - side, they're walk - ing in the
plo - ring, in the sum-mer coun - try - side, they're walk - ing in the
plo - ring, in the sum-mer coun - try - side, they're walk - ing in the
38
poco ritard.
a tempo
p
laz - y sun - shine through the sum-mer coun-try - side.
laz - y sun - shine through the sum-mer coun-try - side.
laz - y sun - shine through the sum-mer coun-try - side.
laz - y sun - shine through the sum-mer coun-try - side.
poco ritard.
a tempo
p
mf
poco rubato
più moto
♩ = 100

39
f
mp
p
slower ♩=80
mp SOLO IV (low voice)
Down the lane, and through the shad-y trees, there's a
pp
colla voce
40
field where the grass rip-ples in the sum-mer breeze; and lit-tle hous-es stand-ing
gradual slow down
cresc.
mf
3
f
there - hous-es with-out win-dows to wel-come the sun and the air, all in rows they
p
mp
mf

(SOLO IV)
FULL
S pp
stand there! Why do they stand there? Why do they stand there?
A pp
Why do they stand there?
T pp
Why do they stand there?
B pp
Why do they stand there?
sf
pp
free time
SPOKEN SOLO (forte)
Suddenly a crow, sitting in a tree, replied:
fff
no Ped.
rhythmic ♩= 80
f CROW (salesman-type)
41
These are the hous-es of our mod-ern coun-try-side! Per-fect for birds who don't
f
p

need to sing or fly! With all mod-cons they don't have to see the sky, all they have to do is to
sit there, lie there, live there, die there...
mf
p
pp
FULL
S p sighing
Hey - ho!
A p sighing
Hey - ho!
T p sighing
Hey - ho!
B p sighing
Hey - ho!
fast and thumping 𝅗𝅥 = 120
42
f
ff
Ped.

f
Hey-ho, the bat-ter-y farm, the hens all in a row;
43
Hey-ho, the but-ter-y farm, the hens they are a-lay-ing O, a-lay-ing
ff
O!

SOLO I
'Which came first? The chick-en or the egg?' Asked Mis-sis Went-worth Brews-ter; 'It
was-n't the chick-en, and it was-n't the egg: it was me! Said the old red roost-er.
44
FULL
Hey - ho, the
Hey - ho, the
Hey - ho, the
Hey - ho, the
44
bat-ter-y farm, the hens all in a row; Hey - ho, the
bat-ter-y farm, the hens all in a row; Hey - ho, the
bat-ter-y farm, the hens all in a row; Hey - ho, the
bat-ter-y farm, the hens all in a row; Hey - ho, the

45

bat-ter-y farm, the hens they are a - lay-ing O, a - lay - ing

bat-ter-y farm, the hens they are a - lay-ing O, a - lay - ing

bat-ter-y farm, the hens they are a - lay-ing O, a - lay - ing

bat-ter-y farm, the hens they are a - lay-ing O, a - lay - ing

45

ff O! ___ *mf* Cock-a-doo-dle doo!

ff O! ___ *mf* Cock-a-doo-dle doo!

ff O! ___ *mf* Cock-a-doo-dle doo!

ff O! ___ *mf* Cock-a-doo-dle doo!

ff *mf*

p Cock-a-doo-dle oo-dle oo-dle oo-dle oo-dle oo-dle oo-dle - oo! ___ *f*

SOLO II *f* I

p Cock-a-doo-dle oo-dle oo-dle oo-dle oo-dle oo-dle oo-dle - oo! ___ *f*

p Cock-a-doo-dle oo-dle oo-dle oo-dle oo-dle oo-dle oo-dle - oo! ___ *f*

p Cock-a-doo-dle oo-dle oo-dle oo-dle oo-dle oo-dle oo-dle - oo! ___ *f*

p *f*

46
said I'd go to work on an egg! They all laughed when I tried it; They
p
said 'You're meant to eat the egg, You're not sup-posed to ride it!'
FULL
47
f
Hey - ho, the bat-ter-y farm, the hens all in a row;
Hey - ho, the bat-ter-y farm, the hens all in a row;
Hey - ho, the bat-ter-y farm, the hens all in a row;
Hey - ho, the bat-ter-y farm, the hens all in a row;
47

Hey - ho, the bat-ter-y farm, the hens they are a - lay - ing O, a - lay - ing
Hey - ho, the bat-ter-y farm, the hens they are a - lay - ing O, a - lay - ing
Hey - ho, the bat-ter-y farm, the hens they are a - lay - ing O, a - lay - ing
Hey - ho, the bat-ter-y farm, the hens they are a - lay - ing O, a - lay - ing
ff
O!
O!
O!
O!
48
48
mf
Cock-a-doo-dle doo!
Cock-a-doo-dle oo-dle oo-dle
Cock-a-doo-dle doo!
Cock-a-doo-dle oo-dle oo-dle
Cock-a-doo-dle doo!
Cock-a-doo-dle oo-dle oo-dle
Cock-a-doo-dle doo!
Cock-a-doo-dle oo-dle oo-dle

oo-dle oo-dle oo-dle oo-dle - oo!
oo-dle oo-dle oo-dle oo-dle - oo!
oo-dle oo-dle oo-dle oo-dle - oo!
oo-dle oo-dle oo-dle oo-dle - oo!
SOLO III
49
Un-cle Bill made Eas-ter Eggs, but he soon gave up his bus-'ness; when he
op-en'd one up, and a ro-bin jump'd out, and wished him Mer-ry Christ-mas!

FULL
50
Hey - ho, the bat-ter-y farm, the hens all in a row;
Hey - ho, the bat-ter-y farm, the hens they are a - lay-ing O, a - lay - ing
O! Cock-a-doo-dle doo! Cock-a-doo-dle oo-dle oo-dle-
clattering

51
oo!
oo!
oo!
oo!
51
SOLO IV
f
You can't make an om'-let and not break eggs! But Aun-tie Mai-sy
p
52
tried it; she blew up an egg with a bi-cy-cle pump, and then she climbed in-side it!

FULL
Hey - ho, the bat-ter-y farm, the hens all in a row;
Hey - ho, the bat-ter-y farm, the hens all in a row;
Hey - ho, the bat-ter-y farm, the hens all in a row;
Hey - ho, the bat-ter-y farm, the hens all in a row;
53
Hey - ho, the bat-ter-y farm, the hens they are a - lay-ing O, a - lay - ing
Hey - ho, the bat-ter-y farm, the hens they are a - lay-ing O, a - lay - ing
Hey - ho, the bat-ter-y farm, the hens they are a - lay-ing O, a - lay - ing
Hey - ho, the bat-ter-y farm, the hens they are a - lay-ing O, a - lay - ing
53
O!
O!
O!
O!

Cock-a-doo-dle doo!
Cock-a-doo-dle doo!
Cock-a-doo-dle oo-dle oo-dle
oo-dle oo-dle oo-dle oo-dle - oo!
Cock-a-doo-dle - doo!
54
SOLO V
Why did the chick-en cross the road? I think she went a-

55
woo - ing; 'cos on the o-ther side she heard a cock a-doo-dle - doo - ing!
FULL
ff
Hey - ho, the bat-ter-y farm, the hens all in a row; —
Hey - ho, the bat-ter-y farm, the hens all in a row; —
Hey - ho, the bat-ter-y farm, the hens all in a row; —
Hey - ho, the bat-ter-y farm, the hens all in a row; —
poco ritard.
a tempo
Hey - ho, the bat-ter-y farm, the hens they are a - lay-ing O, a -
Hey - ho, the bat-ter-y farm, the hens they are a - lay-ing O, a -
Hey - ho, the bat-ter-y farm, the hens they are a - lay-ing O, a -
Hey - ho, the bat-ter-y farm, the hens they are a - lay-ing O, a -
poco ritard.
a tempo

56
fff
luy - ing O!
luy - ing O!
luy - ing O!
luy - ing O!
56
fff
Ped.
Ped.
Ped.
Moderate ♩= 72
CROW (or small group)
mf
So trust in us who know! Those
f
f
p
no Ped.
soft Ped.

57
sim-ple farm-yard crea-tures are not dis - con-tent - ed with their
lot! They give their lives for you, it's true, they're at your beck and call; but
if they did-n't live for you, they would-n't live at all, at all, at all!
mf
faster ♩= 90
f
FULL
S p
All crea-tures
A p
All crea-tures
T p
All crea-tures
B p
All crea-tures
Voices alone ad lib.
mf
sf
f
p

58
f
mf
now in field and farm, give praise to Man who keeps and feeds us.
now in field and farm, give praise to Man who keeps and feeds us.
now in field and farm, give praise to Man who keeps and feeds us.
now in field and farm, give praise to Man who keeps and feeds us.
58
He shields us all from ev-'ry harm, un - til to Death he gent-ly leads us.
He shields us all from ev-'ry harm, un - til to Death he gent-ly leads us.
He shields us all from ev-'ry harm, un - til to Death he gent-ly leads us.
He shields us all from ev-'ry harm, un - til to Death he gent-ly leads us.
59
Man is our guard-ian and our guide, in barn and byre, in sty and stall;
Man is our guard-ian and our guide, in barn and byre, in sty and stall;
Man is our guard-ian and our guide, in barn and byre, in sty and stall;
Man is our guard-ian and our guide, in barn and byre, in sty and stall;
59

his race went forth and mul-ti - plied, and we must die to feed them
his race went forth and mul-ti - plied, and we must die to feed them
his race went forth and mul-ti - plied, and we must die to feed them
his race went forth and mul-ti - plied, and we must die to feed them
60
all.
all.
all.
all.
60
Ped. Ped. Ped. simile
Young sheep for Him be-come roast
Young sheep for Him be-come roast
Young sheep for Him be-come roast
Young sheep for Him be-come roast

lamb, and birds will tum-ble from the sky; for Him the
lamb, and birds will tum-ble from the sky; for Him the
lamb, and birds will tum-ble from the sky; for Him the
lamb, and birds will tum-ble from the sky; for Him the
mf
61
pigs will turn to ham, and cows to steak and
pigs will turn to ham, and cows to steak and
pigs will turn to ham, and cows to steak and
pigs will turn to ham, and cows to steak and
61
kid - ney pie. So let us all give thanks to
kid - ney pie. So let us all give thanks to
kid - ney pie. So let us all give thanks to
kid - ney pie. So let us all give thanks to
p
Ped.

62
Man, and praise Him now while we are a - ble; — we live ac - cord-ing to His
Man, and praise Him now while we are a - ble; — we live ac - cord-ing to His
Man, and praise Him now while we are a - ble; — we live ac - cord-ing to His
Man, and praise Him now while we are a - ble; — we live ac - cord-ing to His
62
riten.
a tempo
plan, and glad - ly die — to grace His ta - ble.
plan, and glad - ly die — to grace His ta - ble.
plan, and glad - ly die — to grace His ta - ble.
plan, and glad - ly die — to grace His ta - ble.
riten.
a tempo
Ped.
Ped.
Ped. simile
dim.
63
ritard.
strict tempo ♩ = 90
CROW
And yet, come all you a-ni-mals, lis-ten to

poco riten.
me! You and your far-mers face re - dun-dun-cy! For there are
quicker ♩= 120
CROW (or small group of 'scientists')
de - di - ca - ted men in sci - en - ti - fic labs, with
simile
64
ar-ti-fi-cial wheat and meat in lit-tle slabs, syn - the-tic-fi-bre-men, whose
heads are al-ways full of the quest for the best
sub - sti - tute for wool; And tech - no - cra - tic wiz - ards who are

poco a poco cresc.
ca-pa-ble and keen, turn-ing grass in-to milk with a mar-vel-lous ma-chine! There are
poco a poco cresc.
65
ar-ti-fi-cial-tim-ber-men pro-du-cing in a flash the
years and years of grow-ing of the oak and of the ash; when com-
pu-ters run the coun-try-side ac-cord-ing to their plan, there
won't be an-y place in it for an-i-mal or man!
f
mf
sf
6
Ped.

FULL
molto riten. Nostalgic swing ♩= 100
66
So make the most of the wheat waving in the fields, it won't be here much longer, it won't be here much longer, it won't be here for long. So make the most of the grass rip-pling in the breeze, it won't be here much

67

long - er, it won't be here much long - er, it won't be here for long.

long - er, it won't be here much long - er, it won't be here for long.

long - er, it won't be here much long - er, it won't be here for long.

long - er, it won't be here much long - er, it won't be here for long.

67

sonoro

mf

Sheep graz - ing, cows moo - ing, the birds' good - morn - ing song,

mf

Sheep graz - ing, cows moo - ing, the birds' good - morn - ing song,

mf

Sheep graz - ing, cows moo - ing, the birds' good - morn - ing song,

mf

sonoro

68 riten.

f

seed for sow - ing, earth for grow - ing, it won't be here for long, so make the

f

seed for sow - ing, earth for grow - ing, it won't be here for long, so make the

f

seed for sow - ing, earth for grow - ing, it won't be here for long, so make the

f

seed for sow - ing, earth for grow - ing, it won't be here for long, so make the

68 riten.

f

a tempo
most of the wheat waving in the fields, it won't be here much long-er,
most of the wheat waving in the fields, it won't be here much long-er,
most of the wheat waving in the fields, it won't be here much long-er,
most of the wheat waving in the fields, it won't be here much long-er,
a tempo
riten.
a tempo
it won't be here much long-er, it won't be here for long.
it won't be here much long-er, it won't be here for long.
it won't be here much long-er, it won't be here for long.
it won't be here much long-er, it won't be here for long.
riten.
a tempo
mf
69
p
mm
p
mm
p
mm
p
mm
69
p
sonoro

(half-closed mouth)
ah
riten.
mf
So make the
a tempo
70
most of the wheat waving in the fields,
it won't be here much
longer, it won't be here much longer,
molto riten.
p
it won't be here for

lilting ♩= 90
poco riten.
long.
long.
long.
long.
lilting ♩= 90
poco riten.
mf
p
Ped.
poco più moto ♩= 100
71
optional cut to 'STEADY'
mf
poco stringendo
p
sonoro
mf
più stringendo
p
steady ♩= 90
f SOLO I
72
SOLO II
SOLO III
Look! There's a house! Up on the hill! Look! There are sta-tues, and
mf
p
poco marcato

SOLO IV
SOLO V (a 'know-all')
SOLO VI (a romantic)
foun-tains, and swans! A stone col-on-ade! And lawns like vel-vet where
sonoro
pea-cocks par-ade!
move on
quicken next four bars starting at ♩=100
HALF CHORUS mf
What are they
SOLO I f
Look! There's a crowd!
move on
quicken next four bars starting at ♩=100
mf
cresc.
73
do-ing? What are they do-ing?
HALF CHORUS
mf
What are they do-ing? What are they do-ing?
f
73
f
steady ♩=90
SOLO IV (grouser)
f
They're do-ing what crowds are al-ways do-ing... queu-ing!
mf
mf
p

slide into
Gavotte ♩= 112
mf
grazioso
SOLO (A Stately-home Guide)
f
This way please, to view the state-ap-part-ments; this way please, you'll
p
74
have to join the queue! This way please, to see the mar-ble fire-place, and
S f
Oh! Here's the ac-tual sword, look,
A f
Oh! Here's the ac-tual sword, look,
here's the ac-tual sword that saved the Duke at Wa-ter-loo!
T f
Oh! Here's the ac-tual sword, look,
B f
Oh! Here's the ac-tual sword, look,
più marziale
f

here's the ac-tual sword, yes, here's the ac-tual sword that saved the Duke at Wa-ter-loo!
here's the ac-tual sword, yes, here's the ac-tual sword that saved the Duke at Wa-ter-loo!
here's the ac-tual sword, yes, here's the ac-tual sword that saved the Duke at Wa-ter-loo!
here's the ac-tual sword, yes, here's the ac-tual sword that saved the Duke at Wa-ter-loo!
75
GUIDE
This way please, and
mf
p
don't walk on the car - pet! This way please, to see the sil-ver spoons.

impressively, but not loud
This way please, up there's the min-strel's gal-ler-y, and here is where the ghost walks on
pp
FULL
76
S pp
Here is where the ghost walks, Here is where the ghost walks,
A pp
Here is where the ghost walks, Here is where the ghost walks,
Tues-day af-ter-noons. Here is where the ghost walks, Here is where the ghost walks,
T pp
B pp
Here is where the ghost walks, Here is where the ghost walks,
76
mf
pp
Here is where the ghost walks on Tues-day af-ter-noons!
Here is where the ghost walks on Tues-day af-ter-noons!
Here is where the ghost walks on Tues-day af-ter-noons!
Here is where the ghost walks on Tues-day af-ter-noons!
ppp
mf
grazioso

GUIDE
This way please, to see the lions and ti - gers;
Oh yes, let's see the
Oh yes, let's see the
this way please, to our Sa-fa-ri Park! Oh yes, let's see the
FULL
Oh yes, let's see the
77
lions and the ti - gers,
Ga-
lions and the ti - gers,
Ga-
GUIDE
FULL
lions and the ti - gers, Ga-zelles, gi-raffes and mon-keys, the dol-phin and the shark! Ga-
lions and the ti - gers,
Ga-
77

zelles, gi-raffes and mon-keys, the dol-phin and the shark, let's see the lions and ti-gers kept in
their Sa-fa-ri Park.
From here on the Solo voices represent
Guides everywhere vanishing into the distance.
SOLO
mf
This way please,
this way please!
mf grazioso
78
p
This way
this way please,
this way

dim.
please, this way please, this way please!
dim.
this way please, this way please!
dim.
please, this way please, this way please!
p
pp
pp
pp
79
79a
mp sonoro
pp
both Ped....
slow ♩ = 56
p SOLO IV
What will be here I wonder, a hundred years from now?
p
sonoro

FULL moderato ♩ = 108
S mf
Car-parks and con-crete, con-crete and car parks, and roads a hun-dred miles
A mf
Car-parks and con-crete, con-crete and car parks, and roads a hun-dred miles
p tranquillo
wide, ho - tels and mo-tels, and mo - tels and ho-tels, and the
wide, ho - tels and mo-tels, and mo - tels and ho-tels, and the
80
cars will go round and round and round, in the con-crete coun - try -
cars will go round and round and round, in the con-crete coun - try -
80

poco ten.

side, in the concrete coun - try - side.

poco ten.

side, in the concrete coun - try - side.

poco

p cresc.

mf

FULL

T mf

Tar-mac and lay-bys, lay-bys and tar-mac, an end - less ston - y

B mf

Tar-mac and lay-bys, lay-bys and tar-mac, an end - less ston - y

p tranquillo

tide, with thou-sands of road signs and drive-ins and snack-bars, and the

tide, with thou-sands of road signs and drive-ins and snack-bars, and the

cars will go round and round and round, in the con-crete coun - try-
cars will go round and round and round, in the con-crete coun - try-

molto riten. 82

S mf
in the con-crete coun - try - side.
pp

A mf
in the con-crete coun - try - side.
pp

T
side, in the con-crete coun - try - side.
pp

B
side, in the con-crete coun - try - side.
pp

molto riten. 82

pp

attacca

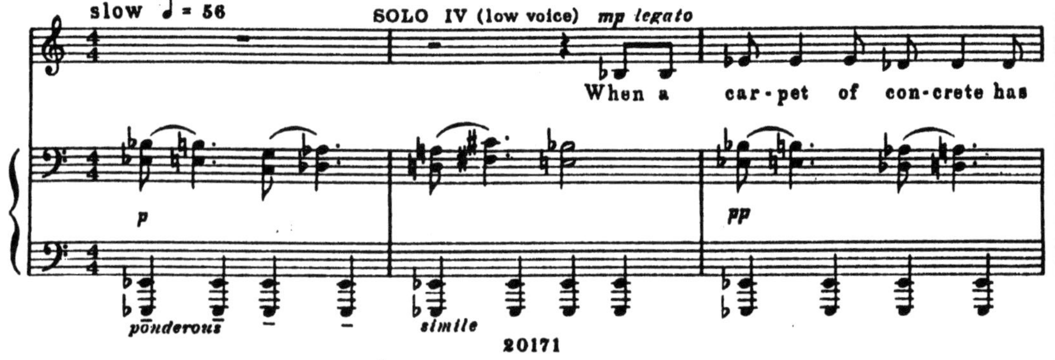
slow ♩ = 56
SOLO IV (low voice) mp legato
When a car-pet of con-crete has
p
pp
ponderous
simile

cov-er'd the land, and Man in his car has dri-ven to ob-liv-ion,

mf dry

HALF CHORUS

SOLO IV

out, from the ru-ins of state-ly Sa-fa-ri Parks, out, from the

mp

83

HALF CHORUS

SOLO IV

cresc.

ru-ins of cir-cus-es and zoos, out, from the lairs where they

cresc.

ff

poco accel.

hide, the li-ons will stride!

molto cresc.

sff

sff

f

Ped. * Ped. * Ped. * Ped. * Ped. *

heavy pounding 𝅗𝅥 = 69
FULL
S
A
T
B
All the li-ons,
all the li-ons, the ti-gers and the mon-keys and the e-le-gant ga-zelle, will
84
leap and roar and roam through the con-crete coun-try-

p
side, through the con-crete coun-try-side! And the
p
side, through the con-crete coun-try-side! And the
p
side, through the con-crete coun-try-side! And the
p
side, through the con-crete coun-try-side! And the
marcato
molto dim.
p
slightly faster 𝅗𝅥=72
cresc.
grass will thrust, and the con-crete crack, and the trees will grow a-
cresc.
grass will thrust, and the con-crete crack, and the trees will grow a-
cresc.
grass will thrust, and the con-crete crack, and the trees will grow a-
cresc.
grass will thrust, and the con-crete crack, and the trees will grow a-
slightly faster 𝅗𝅥=72
sf
simile
mf
85
cresc.
gain; there'll be a mil-lion trees in the jun-gle of Eng-land, a mil-lion trees in the
mf
cresc.
gain; there'll be a mil-lion trees in the jun-gle of Eng-land, a mil-lion trees in the
mf
cresc.
gain; there'll be a mil-lion trees in the jun-gle of Eng-land, a mil-lion trees in the
mf
cresc.
gain; there'll be a mil-lion trees in the jun-gle of Eng-land, a mil-lion trees in the
mf
85
cresc.

jun-gle of Eng - land, and on - ly green will be seen, when the
jun-gle of Eng - land, and on - ly green will be seen, when the
jun-gle of Eng - land, and on - ly green will be seen, when the
jun-gle of Eng - land, and on - ly green will be seen, when the
li - on is king, when the li - on is king, when the li - on rules the
li - on is king, when the li - on is king, when the li - on rules the
li - on is king, when the li - on is king, when the li - on rules the
li - on is king, when the li - on is king, when the li - on rules the
86
poco ritard.
land!
land!
land!
land!
86
poco ritard.

heavy pounding 𝅗𝅥 = 69
ff
All the li-ons, all the ti-gers and the mon-keys and the
All the li-ons, all the ti-gers and the mon-keys and the
All the li-ons, all the li-ons, the ti-gers and the mon-keys and the
All the li-ons, all the li-ons, the ti-gers and the mon-keys and the
heavy pounding 𝅗𝅥 = 69
ff
e-le-gant ga-zelle, will leap and roar and stride — in the deep dark king-dom of the
e-le-gant ga-zelle, will leap and roar and stride — in the deep dark king-dom of the
e-le-gant ga-zelle, will leap and roar and stride — in the deep dark king-dom of the
e-le-gant ga-zelle, will leap and roar and stride — in the deep dark king-dom of the
87
mf
slightly faster 𝅗𝅥 = 72
green, — in the deep dark king-dom of the green! And the grass grows high, and the
green, — in the deep dark king-dom of the green! And the grass grows high, and the
green, — in the deep dark king-dom of the green! And the grass grows high, and the
green, — in the deep dark king-dom of the green! And the grass grows high, and the
87
slightly faster 𝅗𝅥 = 72
marcato
molto dim. p

f
ea-gles cry, and the lion is free a - gain; there'll be a mil - lion lions in the
f
ea-gles cry, and the lion is free a - gain; there'll be a mil - lion lions in the
f
ea-gles cry, and the lion is free a - gain; there'll be a mil - lion lions in the
f
ea-gles cry, and the lion is free a - gain; there'll be a mil - lion lions in the
mf
simile
cresc.
jun-gle of Eng - land, a mil - lion lions in the jun-gle of Eng - land, and
cresc.
jun-gle of Eng - land, a mil - lion lions in the jun-gle of Eng - land, and
cresc.
jun-gle of Eng - land, a mil - lion lions in the jun-gle of Eng - land, and
cresc.
jun-gle of Eng - land, a mil - lion lions in the jun-gle of Eng - land, and
cresc.
88
ff
on - ly green will be seen, when the li-on is king, when the li-on is king,
ff
on - ly green will be seen, when the li-on is king, when the li-on is king.
ff
on - ly green will be seen, when the li-on is king, when the li-on is king,
ff
on - ly green will be seen, when the li-on is king, when the li-on is king,
88
f
sf

move on towards end

when the li - on rules the

when the li - on rules the

when the li - on rules the

when the li - on rules the

move on towards end

sff *sff* *sff*

fff 89

land! ___

fff land! ___

fff land! ___

fff land! ___

89

fff real hot!

sfff

slow ♩= 50 *mf* SOLO IV (low voice)

Mean-while, the lions lie sleep-ing... as the sun goes

pp molto legato

soft Ped. throughout

down, and the Sun-day cars are creep-ing back to the con-crete town.
90
calm ♩ = 42
FULL
S
A
T
B
p delicately
*The cur-few tolls the knell of part-ing day, — The low-ing herd wind
90
calm ♩ = 42
Voices alone ad lib.
slow-ly o'er the lea, — The plow-man home-ward plods his wear-y way, And leaves the

* The words between the asterisks are quoted from Thomas Gray's *Elegy written in a country churchyard.*

with generous sweep ♩= 60
mp
world to dark-ness and to me.* The cur-few tolls the knell of Tho-mas Gray, the
world to dark-ness and to me.* The cur-few tolls the knell of Tho-mas Gray, the
world to dark-ness and to me.* The cur-few tolls the knell of Tho-mas Gray, the
world to dark-ness and to me.* The cur-few tolls the knell of Tho-mas Gray, the
with generous sweep ♩= 60
91
trac-tors now wind slow-ly o'er the lea, the Sun-day dri-ver home-ward plods his
trac-tors now wind slow-ly o'er the lea, the Sun-day dri-ver home-ward plods his
trac-tors now wind slow-ly o'er the lea, the Sun-day dri-ver home-ward plods his
trac-tors now wind slow-ly o'er the lea, the Sun-day dri-ver home-ward plods his
91
mf ten.
more deliberate
p drifting
molto ritard.
way, and leaves the world to dark-ness, to dark-ness...
way, and leaves the world to dark-ness, to dark-ness... to dark - ness..
way, and leaves the world to dark-ness, to dark-ness... to dark - ness..
way, and leaves the world to dark-ness, to dark - ness..
ten.
more deliberate
molto ritard.
mf
sf
mp
p
pp
no arpeggio

slowly flowing ♩= 60

p

Sun - day, ——

pp

pp

pp

slowly flowing ♩= 60

mp

92

good-bye sum-mer

p

Sun - day, ——

good-bye sum-mer

p

Sun - day,

pp

mm ——

p

Sun - day, ——

92

p
Sun - day; day - light go - ing,
Sun - day; day - light go - ing,
Sun - day; day - light go - ing,
p
good-bye Sun-day, day - light go - ing,
93
red sky glow-ing, good - bye sum-mer Sun - day,
red sky glow-ing, good - bye sum-mer Sun - day,
red sky glow-ing, good - bye sum-mer Sun - day,
red sky glow-ing, good - bye sum-mer Sun - day,
93

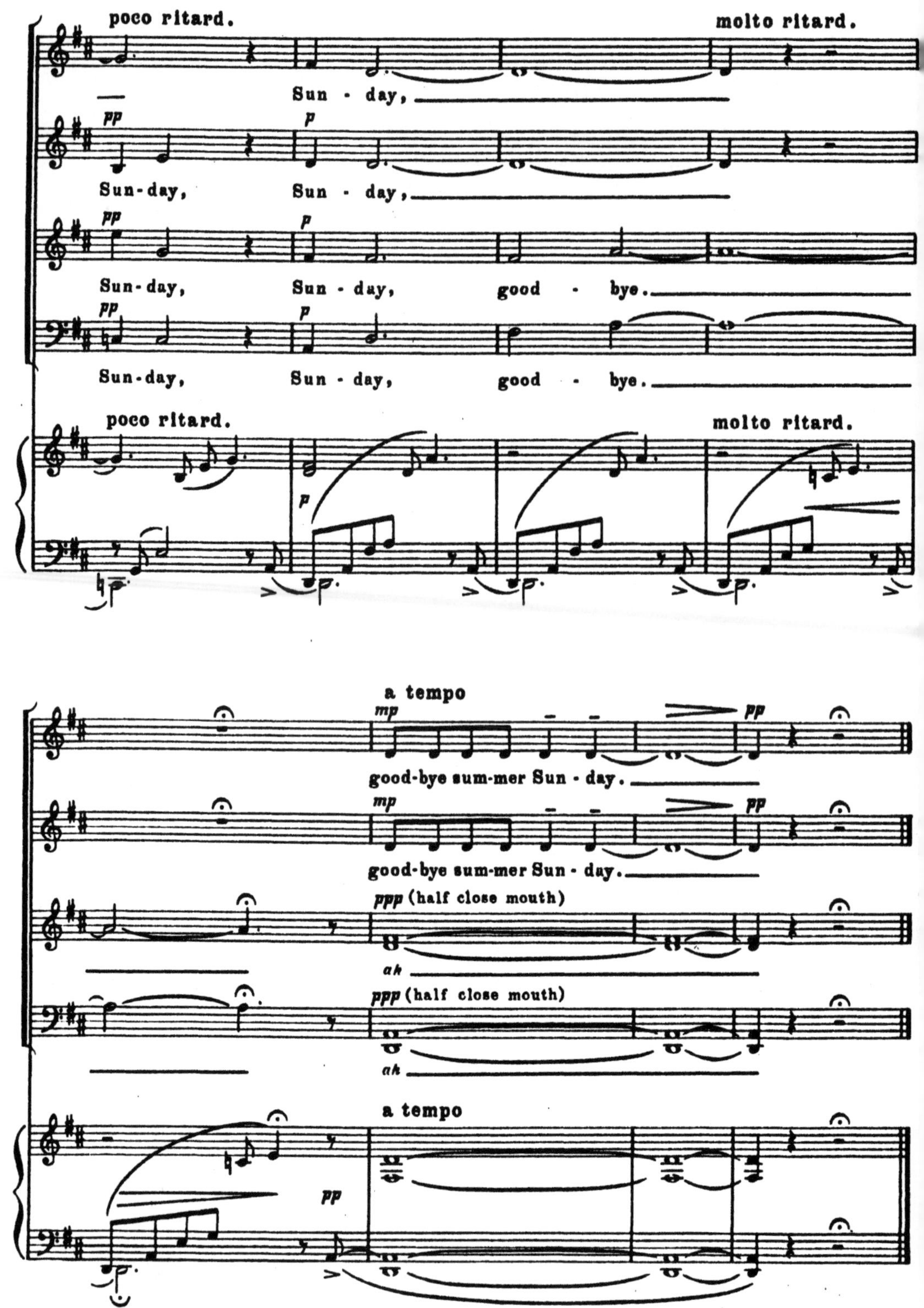

poco ritard.
molto ritard.
Sun - day,
pp
p
Sun-day,
Sun - day,
pp
p
Sun-day,
Sun - day,
good - bye.
pp
p
Sun-day,
Sun - day,
good - bye.
poco ritard.
molto ritard.
p
a tempo
mp
pp
good-bye sum-mer Sun - day.
mp
pp
good-bye sum-mer Sun - day.
ppp (half close mouth)
ah
ppp (half close mouth)
ah
a tempo
pp